# The Golfer's Guide to Life

# The Golfer's Guide to Life

## Players and Philosophers Discuss Life and Links

*Compiled and Edited by Criswell Freeman*

WALNUT GROVE PRESS
Nashville, TN 37205

ISBN 1-887655-38-7

*The ideas expressed in this book are not, in all cases, exact quotations, as some have been edited for clarity and brevity. In all cases, the author has attempted to maintain the speaker's original intent. In some cases, material for this book was obtained from secondary sources, primarily print media. While every effort was made to ensure the accuracy of these sources, the accuracy cannot be guaranteed. For additions, deletions, corrections or clarifications in future editions of this text, please write WALNUT GROVE PRESS.*

Printed in the United States of America
Cover Design by Mary Mazer
Typesetting & Page Layout by Sue Gerdes
Editor for Walnut Grove Press: Alan Ross
3 4 5 6 7 8 9 10 •      99 00 01

ACKNOWLEDGMENTS
The author gratefully acknowledges the helpful support of Angela Beasley, Dick and Mary Freeman, and Mary Susan Freeman.

*For Virginia Criswell*

A Lifetime Supporter On and Off the Links

# Table of Contents

# Introduction

Since a fateful day in 1963 when my dad came home with a paper bag containing four used clubs, I have been fascinated by golf. As a young boy, the game was simple: Swing away and hope. But as I matured, I began to appreciate the subtleties and beauty of the sport. Gradually, I came to the same realization that has touched the lives of countless duffers and pros alike: Golf is an awful lot like life.

Lee Trevino declared, "Golf is the most human game of all." Perhaps this helps explain the game's enduring popularity.

This book outlines ten principles which apply on the links or off. In support of these ideas, I have selected quotations from a collection of great golfers and great thinkers. These principles, properly applied, may help lower your handicap — if so, that's good. But more importantly, these principles apply to the game that is played beyond the 18th green.

As you consider the words that follow, examine your own style of play. If you've been a believer in the "swing away and hope" method, reconsider. After all, whether it's the game of golf or the game of life, it's always a good time to improve your score.

# LESSON 1: LIFETIME LEARNING
## *Take a Lesson*

The Stoic philosopher Epictetus observed, "No great thing is created suddenly." And so it is with a golf swing. Proper technique may take years to achieve and a lifetime to master. That's why the serious golfer understands that his education is ongoing.

Jack Nicklaus, perhaps the greatest golfer ever to swing a club, advised, "Don't be afraid to take a lesson. I'm not."

And if it's good enough for the Golden Bear, it's good enough for the rest of us.

Always keep learning.
It keeps you young.

*Patty Berg*

Learn from the skillful.
He who teaches himself,
hath a fool for his master.

*Ben Franklin*

It takes twenty years to make
an overnight success.

*Eddie Cantor*

You must work very hard to become
a natural golfer.

*Gary Player*

It is easier to learn something new than it is
to unlearn something that you have been
doing wrong for a long time.

*Harvey Penick*

Watch your golf swing on videotape.
In your mind, you may be Fred Couples.
On tape, you may be Fred Mertz.

*Glen Waggoner*

Nothing goes down slower
than a golf handicap.

*Bobby Nichols*

It does not matter how slowly you go
so long as you do not stop.

*Confucius*

He knows enough who knows how to learn.

*Henry Adams*

The average golfer is entirely capable
of building a repeating swing and breaking 80.

*Ben Hogan*

I think that, in golf, your physical and mental
capabilities aren't really compatible
until you're 35 to 45. Those, to me,
are your peak years.

*Raymond Floyd*

I am still learning.

*Michelangelo's Motto*

Golf is a microcosm of this world in which
we live — a game rich in humanity.

*C. Grant Spaeth*

Nothing is impossible to a willing heart.

*John Heywood*

There is nothing in this game of golf that
can't be improved upon — if you practice.

*Patty Berg*

Work to become, not acquire.

*Elbert Hubbard*

Golf is perpetual loss and rediscovery.

*Thomas Boswell*

I probably have forgotten more about golf than I will ever learn. What you do is remember some of the things you thought you'd never forget.

*Jack Nicklaus*

The secret of golf is to get a complex mortal to simplify positions and actions as much as possible.

*Tommy Armour*

The game is most fun when you are experimenting.

*Jack Nicklaus*

Mistakes are their own instructors.

*Horace*

Every cure is temporary. But it's nice while it lasts.

*Jack Nicklaus*

The doer alone learneth.

*Nietzsche*

If you're smart, you learn something from
every round you play.

*Sam Snead*

It takes just as long to play your way out of
a slump as it does to play your way into one.

*Harvey Penick*

Don't consider losses a waste of time.
Consider them an apprenticeship.

*Greg Norman*

Improvement lies in narrowing the margin
between your best and worst shots.

*Jack Nicklaus*

Many amateurs have a tendency to overdo
instruction. It's like the old saying, "A couple
of aspirin might cure what ails you, but the
whole bottle will probably kill you."

*Sam Snead*

All human power is a compound
of time and patience.

*Honoré de Balzac*

What we have to learn to do, we learn
by doing.

*Aristotle*

It is part of the cure to wish to be cured.

*Seneca*

I learned to play golf from Nelson and Hogan,
which is like learning to paint from
Michelangelo and Leonardo.

*Ken Venturi*

When the pupil is ready, the teacher
will come.

*Chinese Saying*

Knowledge is power.

*Francis Bacon*

No man ever became wise by chance.

*Seneca*

Preparation through steady practice
   is the only honest avenue to achieving
         your potential.

*Chi Chi Rodriguez*

# LESSON 2: COURAGE
## *Go for the Green*

Sam Snead, in discussing the topic of golfing courage, recalled an old Virginia adage: "The Good Lord hates a coward, but he's not real fond of a fool, either." These words seem to sum up a grand paradox of golf: Both courage and timidity are often punished.

Whether we're on the links or off, each of us must find a balance between foolish bravado and needless fear. We must decide whether to follow our dreams or to recoil from our worst nightmares. Our choices, taken as a whole, make us who we are. And while there are no hard and fast guidelines, history seems to show that, on balance, courage is its own reward.

Two thousand years ago, Tacitus observed, "The desire for safety stands against every great and noble enterprise." Spoken like a man standing in the fairway of a par five who is about to go for the green in two.

Golf is the
"only-est" sport.
You're completely alone
with every conceivable
opportunity to defeat
yourself.

*Hale Irwin*

The fearful Unbelief is unbelief in yourself.

*Thomas Carlyle*

Great players know how — and when —
to be aggressive.

*Greg Norman*

I feel more comfortable attacking the course
rather than playing it cautiously.

*Arnold Palmer*

All fear is a sign of want of faith.

*Mohandas Gandhi*

Golf may not teach character,
but it reveals it.

*Thomas Boswell*

Golf tells you much about character.
Play a round of golf with someone, and you
know them more intimately than you might
from years of dinner parties.

*Harvey Penick*

Success in golf depends less on strength
of body than upon strength of mind
and character.

*Arnold Palmer*

# Character is destiny.

*Heraclitus*

# Remember golf presents no physical danger.

*Bobby Jones*

The best players fail the most because they are in the hunt all the time.

*Deane Beman*

I think players have a fear of finding out their true limits, which is even greater than their fear of failure.

*Peter Jacobsen*

Ask yourself, "What's the worst that can happen?" Prepare to accept it. Then improve upon the worst.

*Dale Carnegie*

No matter what happens, I can always dig ditches.

*Arnold Palmer*

Some say, "Be patient." Then I hear,
"Just let it happen." Then there are guys who
"make it happen."

*Tom Kite*

The two things that motivate me most
are fear of failure and
a desire for self-improvement.

*Jack Nicklaus*

Trust your hopes, not your fears.

*David Mahoney*

Most golfers prepare for disaster.
A good golfer prepares for success.

*Bob Toski*

I'm not about to quit. You just gotta keep
beating the ball, grit your teeth
and make birdies.

*Jim Thorpe*

Your reach and your grasp should be the
same. That's the way to be happy. Reach
for the furthest thing you think you can get.
Then reach again. Sooner or later, the things
that looked way beyond you are the next
natural goal to reach.

*Calvin Peete*

He conquers who endures.

*Persius*

Keep hitting it straight until the wee ball
goes in the hole.

*James Braid*

The first and great commandment is
don't let them scare you.

*Elmer Davis*

Courage is the price life extracts
for granting peace.

*Amelia Earhart*

A buoyant, positive approach to the game
is as basic as a sound swing.

*Tony Lema*

When in doubt, do the courageous thing.

*Jan Smuts*

# Be decisive.
## A wrong decision is generally less disastrous than indecision.

*Bernhard Langer*

# Happiness is a form of courage.

*Holbrook Jackson*

Faith is in your heart.
Confidence is in your mind
as well as your heart.
In golf, true confidence
will always beat
blind faith.

*Harvey Penick*

Have courage for the
great sorrows of life and
patience for the small
ones; and when you have
laboriously accomplished
your daily task,
go to sleep in peace.
God is awake.

*Victor Hugo*

# LESSON 3: ATTITUDE
## *Believe in Your Swing*

Marcus Aurelius observed, "Man must be arched and buttressed from within, else the temple waivers to the dust." And like a good man or woman, a good golf game depends almost entirely upon inner strength.

Gary Player wrote, "There's absolutely no question that golf is a game of mind over matter." In this chapter, we consider ways to improve one's golf score by improving one's attitude.

All too often, a bogey is simply a physical manifestation of the self-fulfilling prophesy. We become better golfers once we convince ourselves that the same may be said of birdies.

I think that to score
in golf is a matter
of confidence.

*Henry Cotton*

You have more potential than you think.

*Sam Snead*

In my opinion, the average golfer
underestimates himself.

*Ben Hogan*

Self-confidence is the first requisite
to great undertakings.

*Samuel Johnson*

They can because they think they can.

*Virgil*

You are what you think
you are, in golf
and in life.

*Raymond Floyd*

I'm as good a player as
I think I am. If you can't
win in your own dreams,
forget it.

*Calvin Peete*

The hardest thing is to *believe*
that *you* can get to the top.

*Jim Thorpe*

Man is what he believes.

*Anton Chekhov*

My golf game improved when I got better
at believing in myself.

*Dawn Coe-Jones*

Clear your mind of can't.

*Samuel Johnson*

Don't give up on proper thinking just because it doesn't work one day.

*Tom Watson*

The perfect round of golf
has never been played.
It's 18 holes-in-one.
I almost dreamt it once,
but I lipped out at 18.

*Ben Hogan*

When I'm on, golf has no strategy.
I drill every shot at the pin. I want to hole out
from the fairway.

*Lanny Wadkins*

When I'm in a zone, I don't think about the
shot or the wind or the distance or the gallery
or anything; I just pull a club and swing.

*Mark Calcavecchia*

When I play my best golf, I feel as if I'm in
a fog, standing back watching the earth
in orbit with a golf club in my hands.

*Mickey Wright*

You have to train
the mind for success.

*Calvin Peete*

# The best way to build confidence is to succeed.

*Lee Trevino*

Few athletes trust their minds as much
as their muscles.

*Thomas Boswell*

When the great player makes a mistake,
he says, "I'm going to work on that and not do
it again." The bad player says, "Boy, I messed
up again. I guess I really am a dog."

*Peter Jacobsen*

Human thoughts have the tendency to turn
themselves into their physical equivalents.

*Earl Nightingale*

Assume a virtue if you have it not.

*William Shakespeare*

The pessimist complains about the wind;
the optimist expects it to change;
the realist adjusts the sails.

*William Arthur Ward*

My father told me, "You must never learn
to think the negative."

*Johnny Miller*

Whether you think you can
or think you can't, you're right.

*Henry Ford*

Aptitude starts with attitude.

*Greg Norman*

Don't linger too long
in thinking about your
shots — good or bad —
but stamp the good ones
into your mind for
future reference.

*Greg Norman*

The most important thing
for me in preparing for
major tournaments is
basic peace of mind.

*Jack Nicklaus*

If a player is confident in the club he has selected, that confidence is reflected in his swing.

*Cary Middlecoff*

The brain controls the mind.
 The mind controls the body.
 The body controls the club.

*Mike Hebron*

Make up your mind before your backswing
starts, then let your muscles do the work.

*Tommy Armour*

The more time I have to think about a shot,
 the worse I'm going to hit it.

*Larry Laoretti*

The man who insists upon seeing
 with perfect clearness before he decides,
 never decides.

*Henri Frédéric Amiel*

B e yourself. Play your own game.

*Harvey Penick*

S implicity is the answer. I only check
three things — my timing, my balance and
my square hand position at address.

*Calvin Peete*

G o from strength to strength.

*Greg Norman*

G olf is more a game of head and heart
than of guts and muscle.

*Thomas Boswell*

Never think about what you did wrong
on the last shot. Think about what you will do
right on the next one.

*Tommy Armour*

There is nothing final about a mistake,
except its being taken as final.

*Phyliss Bottome*

Our greatest foes, and whom we chiefly
combat, are within.

*Miguel de Cervantes*

Prayer has given me the strength,
concentration and confidence necessary
to perform a seemingly impossible task.

*Dick Chapman,*
*Winner of the 1949 Canadian Amateur*

Golf makes one loathe mediocrity.

*Gary Player*

The fellow who wins is the fellow
who thinks he can win.

*Gay Brewer*

The happiness of your life depends
upon the quality of your thoughts; therefore,
guard accordingly.

*Marcus Aurelius*

Very often, what a man
feels he is doing is
more important than
what he does.

*Bobby Jones*

Golf is 20 percent mechanics and technique. The other 80 percent is philosophy, humor, tragedy, romance, melodrama, companionship, camaraderie, cussedness and conversation.

*Grantland Rice*

# LESSON 4: CONCENTRATION
## *Keep Your Head Down*

Since the better part of golf is played between the ears, it's no accident that the game's most popular adage concerns the human head. All golfers, from time to time, fall prey to the powerful temptation to look up before the swing is completed. The results are predictable: Curiosity kills the cat, or, in this case, the birdie.

In golf, as in life, concentration is rewarded at every turn. When we attend to the job at hand, the game seems to flow. But as distractions increase, so do bogeys.

If you're looking for a surefire way to lower your handicap, learn the fine art of concentration. If you keep your head down during the swing, you can hold your head high after the swing is over.

On the golf course,
concentrate on the
present, forget the past,
and don't look
too far ahead.

*Judy Rankin*

Maintaining your composure on the golf course is worth at least three shots a round.

*Billy Casper*

Some golfers I've met can't achieve total
concentration because they're too brilliant
for their own good. They over-analyze.

*Sam Snead*

When you're afraid, keep your mind on
what you have to do. And if you have been
thoroughly prepared, you will not be afraid.

*Dale Carnegie*

Focus not on the commotion around you
but on the opportunity ahead of you.

*Arnold Palmer*

Become so wrapped up in something
that you forget to be afraid.

*Lady Bird Johnson*

In golf, the hands are the chief point
of concentration.

*Harry Vardon*

This game is like a horse. If you take your
eye off it, it'll jump back and kick your shins.

*Byron Nelson*

At its best, the U. S. Open demands
the patience of St. Francis and the will
of General George Patton.

*Thomas Boswell*

To be disciplined from within, where all
is permissible, where all is concealed —
that is the point.

*Michel de Montaigne*

Golf is you against yourself.

*Jack Nicklaus*

All serious doubts start from within.

*Eudora Welty*

Teach yourself to work in uncertainty.

*Bernard Malamud*

What you think while you're playing golf
is probably the most important single part
of your game.

*Gary Player*

Many golfers can't concentrate because
they're too self-conscious.

*Sam Snead*

Always put score ahead of pride.

*Ken Venturi*

The scoring at golf is as much about
avoiding disasters as making birdies.

*Jack Nicklaus*

Golf is a game of mistakes. The best players
make the smallest mistakes.

*Sam Snead*

Keep your head down, don't visit with anyone during the round, and go about your business.

*Ben Hogan*

# LESSON 5: PREPARATION
## *Groove Your Swing*

The philosopher Epictetus advised his students, "Practice, for heaven's sake, in the little things; and then proceed to greater." Although Epictetus was certainly no golfer, his advice still applies on the links. A sound golf swing is never built overnight. But with consistent effort, small strides on the practice tee produce big results on the score card.

Two thousand years after Epictetus spoke his words, a twenty-nine-year-old accountant named Julius Boros decided to take a chance on the PGA tour. Because he had taken an accountant's care to build a solid swing, Boros quickly earned a reputation for consistency. Eventually, he won two U. S. Opens and a place in the Hall of Fame.

Boros advised, "Think of your golf swing as a machine. Build the most efficient machine you can." If *you* want to build an efficient striking machine, carefully consider each facet of the golf swing. Then groove those fundamentals into your swing on the practice tee. Whether you're an accountant or a philosopher, great things are sure to follow.

My only goal is to improve my golf swing.
Everything else will take care of itself.

*Tom Watson*

I grew up knowing you cannot be a success
in life if you don't work hard.

*Gary Player*

The amount you are willing to work
on your game will determine how much
of your potential you will realize.

*Ken Venturi*

God gives talent. Work transforms
talent into genius.

*Anna Pavlova*

I advocate working hard
on the fundamentals
and then working
the fundamentals
into your game.

*Ben Hogan*

Never lose the will to improve.

*Tom Watson*

Goals are the fuel of progress.

*Greg Norman*

Setting goals is an art. The trick is setting them at the right level — neither too high nor too low.

*Greg Norman*

When a man's willing and eager, the gods join in.

*Aeschylus*

Practice your swing until
it becomes a habit
of mind and muscle.

*Sam Snead*

To learn new habits is everything,
    for it is to reach the substance of life.
        Life is but a tissue of habits.
                                *Henri Frédéric Amiel*

My goal? Consistency.
    I try to do the same thing each time out.
                                *Greg Norman*

The simple swing that is also sound will be
        susceptible to repetition.
                                *Bobby Jones*

Even a flawed swing can be effective
if it is repeatable.

*Cary Middlecoff*


All the vital technical parts of the swing
take place in back of you, or above the head.
It's terrifying to think of all the gremlins that
can creep into your game. The margin
for error is infinitesimal.

*Roger Maltbie*


Once you've grooved your swing,
you shouldn't be conscious of making
any fundamental changes, no matter what
club you are using.

*Ben Hogan*


The best swing is the one that repeats.

*Lee Trevino*

The purpose of the waggle is to avoid and
destroy tension.

*Bobby Jones*

Feel the club.

*Jim Flick*

The waggle gives you the feeling of the club
in your hands.

*Julius Boros*

There is no one, standard, correct grip size
for everyone. It all comes down to feel.

*Ken Venturi*

Good golf begins with a good grip.

*Ben Hogan*

Unless you have a reasonably good grip
and stance, anything you read about the golf
swing is useless.

*Harvey Penick*

A backswing that is too short inevitably
goes with a grip that is too tight.

*Bobby Jones*

The cardinal principle in all golf shot-making
is that if you move your head, you ruin
your body action.

*Tommy Armour*

The key to a good swing
is maintaining balance.

*Gary McCord*

In golf, there is never a single reason
for success.

*Sam Snead*

# My goal is to hit the perfect shot every time I swing at it.

*Tom Watson*

Let your goals be
important enough
to override your
distractions.

*Billy Casper*

I want to make this game easy. Improving my
swing is a simplifying principle. It eliminates
a lot of clutter, a lot of false issues.

*Tom Watson*

A simple tip to improve timing is this:
Pause briefly at the top of the backswing.

*Tommy Armour*

Nobody ever swung a golf club too slowly.

*Bobby Jones*

Unless by pure accident,
no good ever comes
from a bad stroke.

*Harry Vardon*

You'll never learn to play
golf on a golf course.

*Lee Trevino*

To get the most from practice,
> you have to have a plan.

*Sam Snead*

The good player doesn't experiment
> or force changes during a round.

*Ken Venturi*

Practice barefoot sometimes.
> It'll give you a better sense of feel and
> slow down your swing.

*Sam Snead*

What a shame to waste great shots
> on the practice tee.

*Walter Hagen*

There's much more to learning how to hit good golf shots than belting out a few million balls.

*Jack Nicklaus*

# First deserve, then desire.

*English Proverb*

The way to build your swing is through
intelligent practice.

*Cary Middlecoff*

Playing tournament golf without practice
is like walking downstairs in pitch darkness.

*Thomas Boswell*

A faulty swing ties you up so that
a smooth stroke becomes impossible.

*Bobby Jones*

There is only one swing: the correct one.

*Ernest Jones*

A lot of players have the talent but not
the drive to win. There are also guys who want
to be the best and who really work at it, but
who don't have the talent.

*Jack Nicklaus*

People tell me, "You got it made." I know
better. I know where I came from. I've got to
work three times as hard to stay where I am.

*Jim Thorpe*

This game is about as close to the American
Dream as you can get. The harder you work,
the more respect you get.

*John Mahaffey*

Luck is the residue of design.

*Branch Rickey*

You can't go into a golf shop and buy
a good game.

*Sam Snead*

The world took six days. Your golf swing
may take a little longer.

*Glen Waggoner*

He who labors diligently need never despair;
for all things are accomplished
by diligence and labor.

*Menander*

# LESSON 6: SELF-CONTROL
## *As Your Temper Rises, So Does Your Score*

During his heyday, Tommy Bolt's temper was infamous. Bolt could fling a club with the best of them. In fact, Jimmy Demaret proclaimed, "Tommy Bolt's putter had more air time than Lindbergh." But even the mercurial Bolt knew the value of self-control. He once admitted, "It's a game of patience." So much for air-born putters.

Publilius Syrus once observed, "Anger tortures itself." It might be added that on golf courses — or off — runaway emotions are the most dangerous hazards.

Golf is a non-violent
game played violently
from within.

*Bob Toski*

More than any other game, golf is about
self-control, restraint of personality,
and the mastering of the emotions.

*Thomas Boswell*

Over-aggression has never won
a golf tournament.

*Jack Nicklaus*

Have patience with all things, but first of all
with yourself.

*St. Francis of Sales*

Golf may be a sophisticated game.
At least, it is usually played with the outward
appearance of great dignity. It is, nevertheless,
a game of considerable passion, either of the
explosive type, or that which burns inwardly
and sears the soul.

*Bobby Jones*

Patience is power.

*Chinese Proverb*

The most exquisitely satisfying act in the
world of golf is that of throwing a club.
The full backswing, the delayed wrist action,
the flowing follow-through, followed by that
unique whirring sound, reminiscent only
of a flock of passing starlings,
is without parallel in sport.

*Henry Longhurst*

When Arnold Palmer first came on the tour,
he'd throw his clubs *backward*! I taught him to
throw them forward so he could pick them up
on the way.

*Tommy Bolt*

It is the poor craftsman who blames his tools.

*Glen Waggoner*

Trouble once begun may never come
to an end until the card is torn
into a thousand fragments.

*Bernard Darwin*

Golf is the humbling game and none know
that better than the best.

*Thomas Boswell*

A lot of times you don't
actually win so much
as the other guys lose.

*Jack Nicklaus*

Stay in the present tense.

*Tom Kite*

Staying in the present is the key to any golfer's game. Once you start thinking about a shot you just messed up or what you have to do on the next nine to catch somebody, you're lost.

*Paul Azinger*

No man can succeed at golf until he has mastered the art of not permitting one bad hole, or indeed one bad shot, to affect the rest of his game.

*Henry Longhurst*

If you let the last shot interfere with the next one, you cheat yourself.

*Curtis Strange*

To mourn a mischief that
is past and gone
Is the next way to draw
new mischief on.

*William Shakespeare*

When people hear the word *control* in regard to golf, they usually think it means being conservative. I disagree. Being in control means making intelligent decisions — knowing when to be aggressive and when to be cautious.

*Curtis Strange*

Think like a man
of action, act like
a man of thought.

*Henri Bergson*

Society has made us so aware of wanting instant results that people have forgotten the fundamentals that have to be under control before they can succeed, whether it's in business, golf or life.

*Jim Flick*

Never let emotions interfere with the ability to make smart decisions.

*Curtis Strange*

True aggressiveness is based not on self-idolatry or self-pity; it is based on self-knowledge.

*Greg Norman*

Play within yourself — play your own game.

*Billy Casper*

Remember the game is played one stroke at a time. You can't play the next shot until you've played this one.

*Mary Lena Faulk*

He is next to the gods whom reason impels.

*Claudius*

Give it your best, but if somebody beats you fair and square, congratulate him and move on.

*Greg Norman*

The only bruises in golf are to the spirit.

*Thomas Boswell*

There are two things the players on tour should realize: Adults will copy your swing, and young people will follow your example.

*Harvey Penick*

Misfortunes one can endure —
they come from outside, they are accidents.
But to suffer for one's own faults — ah —
there is the sting of life.

*Oscar Wilde*

Do not weep; do not wax indignant.
Understand.

*Baruch Spinoza*

Golf, it has now long since been forgotten,
is essentially a simple pastime wherein you
start at A and hole out at B, overcoming as
best you may such hazards as you encounter
on the way.

*Henry Longhurst*

# LESSON 7: RELAXATION
## *Swing Easy, Hit Hard*

In golf, power is paradoxical. Overswinging destroys both balance and tempo, resulting in decreased accuracy and distance. In the tee box, the law of unintended consequences is alive and well: When we swing too hard, our shots fall short.

Recalling his days on the tour, Byron Nelson noted, "We thought that strength denied touch and that you could not consistently hit the ball long and straight. It's been proved that you can."

The purpose of a golf swing is to develop clubhead speed through the point of impact. This goal is best achieved through smooth acceleration, not quick bursts of energy.

The same principles that provide power on the golf course also make us more effective in other areas of our lives. Life, like that little dimpled golf ball, can't be overpowered. So the best course of action, no matter where we find ourselves, is to swing easy and hit hard.

Overswinging does not produce power.

*Judy Rankin*

No good player ever swings as hard as he can.

*Arnold Palmer*

The length of a drive depends not upon brute force, but upon the speed of the clubhead.

*Bobby Jones*

To hit the ball farther, don't swing faster or harder. Make a fuller, more fluid swing. That's how you get more clubhead speed.

*Beth Daniel*

# Don't press. You can hit hard without pressing.

*Harry Vardon*

Golf is a game based not only on an
intellectual understanding but also on
sensitivity for the instrument. You can't bully
your way to a good golf swing.

*Jim Flick*

Tension is golf's worst enemy.

*Bobby Jones*

Too many people try to overpower
the golf ball like they do their businesses.

*Jim Flick*

Golf is a walk in the park,
not a 400-meter dash.

*Tom Watson*

A controlled shot to a closely guarded
green is the surest test of any man's golf.
*A. W. Tillinghast*

The busier you keep yourself with the details
of a particular shot, the less time your mind
has to dwell on the emotional "ifs" and "buts."
*Jack Nicklaus*

Fear ruins more golf shots
than any other factor.
*Tommy Armour*

We hope vaguely but dread precisely.
*Paul Valéry*

The challenge in a golf stroke is to maintain
a perfect balance between firmness
and relaxation in the interests
of control and rhythm.

*Bobby Jones*

Your ideal tempo is the maximum speed
at which you can control your body
and the club.

*Al Geiberger*

I've always tried to swing at about 85 percent
of my top speed. That's a pace I can control.

*Sam Snead*

Every good golfer possesses a carefully
developed set of key swing thoughts that
he uses to keep his game in balance.

*Jack Nicklaus*

Standing over the shot, put everything
out of your mind except one key technical
thought and a "feel" for timing.

*Sam Snead*

The best cure for the body is to quiet
the mind.

*Napoleon I*

Mental discipline, muscle memory.
   Practice until you don't have to think.

*Calvin Peete*

The chains of habit are too weak to be felt
   until they are too strong to be broken.

*Samuel Johnson*

You have to find a way to rise above —
   or drop below — anxiety. You have to find
   a trance, some kind of self-hypnosis
   that's almost a state of grace.

*Hale Irwin*

I don't go into a trance when I address
   the ball, but I come close.

*Sam Snead*

Confidence comes from hitting enough
good shots that you know you can do it again.
Whistling in the dark is not the answer.

*Harvey Penick*

Education is hanging on
until you've caught on.

*Robert Frost*

Luck is not chance, it's Toil.
Fortune's expensive smile is earned.

*Emily Dickinson*

Start your downswing in a leisurely fashion,
in no hurry coming down, with the
acceleration smooth and natural.

*Bobby Jones*

Lift the club with a light grip, so that it feels
heavy, like using an ax. You don't hit with
an ax, you accelerate it. That is exactly
what you should do with a golf club.

*Peter Thomson*

Hum your favorite waltz and swing
to the beat of the tune.

*Sam Snead*

Tension is the product of technique
or temperament, or both, and it just eats up
the golf swing.

*Sam Snead*

Hit against a firm left side, but hit with
the right side. That's the source of power.

*Calvin Peete*

When it comes time to hit, don't leap at
the ball, but keep on swinging until the ball
has had a good start down the fairway,
and the clubhead has done its job.

*Bobby Jones*

Swing with ease against a breeze.

*Golf Digest Tip*

# Why are our practice swings the best swings? We don't think about the ball, only the flow.

*Ken Venturi*

For a good golf score, anxiety is fatal.

*Cary Middlecoff*

Most golfers are not thinking, even when they believe they are. They are only worrying.

*Harvey Penick*

It's time to stop thinking, stop talking, and start playing.

*Jack Nicklaus*

Blessed are those who forget, for they thus surmount even their own mistakes.

*Nietzsche*

When I swing, my mind is blank, and my body is as loose as a goose.

*Sam Snead*

I don't swing hard.
I hit hard.

*Julius Boros*

# LESSON 8: MATURITY
## *Make Every Shot Count*

Eight centuries before the birth of Christ, the Greek poet Hesiod advised, "It is best to do things systematically since we are only human, and disorder is our worst enemy." His advice applies to life and links.

More recently, Jack Nicklaus asked, "How many shots would you have saved if you never lost your temper, never got down on yourself, always developed strategy before hitting, and always played within your capabilities?" Most of us are too embarrassed to answer.

The game of golf rewards maturity. So does the game of life. Plan accordingly.

On every hole, never tee it up
without a plan.

*Julius Boros*

Good people order and arrange.

*Confucius*

Action before thought is the ruination
of most of your shots.

*Tommy Armour*

Imagine first that the present is past and,
second, that the past may yet be changed
and amended.

*Viktor Frankl*

You must be thoughtful if you want to get
ahead in golf.

*Harry Vardon*

After you've grooved your swing,
you still have to master the tactics of getting
around the course. A good swing is small
satisfaction if you can't break 100.

*Sam Snead*

I never hit a shot, even in practice,
without having a very sharp in-focus picture
of it in my head.

*Jack Nicklaus*

Always visualize your shot.

*Ken Venturi*

Don't just play your way around the course. *Think* your way around the course.

*Sam Snead*

The key to golf is to play the ball to the best position from which to play the next shot.

*Arnold Palmer*

Course management is like being in a chess game. You're maneuvering for position.

*Patty Sheehan*

Every shot has its own risk/reward factor.

*Tom Watson*

Play the shot you've got the greatest chance of playing well.

*Tommy Armour*

A golf course is never quite the same from one day to the next. So you have to be able to meet the course on *its* terms, not your own.

*Billy Casper*

Preparing yourself for the course
you're about to play is a big part
of course management.

*Billy Casper*

Forewarned, forearmed; to be prepared
is half the victory.

*Miguel de Cervantes*

The essence of knowledge is, having it,
to use it.

*Confucius*

Great players learn that they don't need
to play their best golf to win. They only need
to shoot the lowest score.

*Tom Watson*

The best strategic advice is this: Know your strengths and take advantage of them.

*Greg Norman*

Don't be afraid to be patient.

*Curtis Strange*

Something really clicked on the day I finally discovered the meaning of playing within myself. Ever since, the game has seemed a lot easier.

*Tiger Woods*

Every golfer scores better when he learns his capabilities.

*Tommy Armour*

Don't be ashamed to play safe.

*Arnold Palmer*

There's no rule in golf that states
"thou shall shoot for the flagstick."

*Patty Sheehan*

The champion is the fellow who can make
the fewest poor shots.

*Tommy Armour*

The only thing that can get in the way
of a golfer's success is the golfer himself.

*Billy Casper*

One of the worst mistakes you can make
in golf is trying to *force* the game.

*Jack Nicklaus*

The best advice I can give any golfer about playing fairway shots is:
Don't be greedy.

*Gary Player*

Every hole is a little tournament of its own.

*Tom Watson*

The strategy of a golf course is the soul
of the game.

*George Thomas, Jr.*

The final round of the U. S. Open is not
so much a test of golf as a test of judgment.

*Jack Nicklaus*

Golf is like chess. You have to think ahead.
Plot the hole back from the flag.

*Tom Watson*

I have seen many really good players
    attempt shots they should have known
        were impossible.

*Bobby Jones*

To attempt the impossible is always a fault;
    to do so repeatedly is fatal.

*Machiavelli*

You don't have to hit the ball perfectly to win;
    you have to manage yourself better.

*Tom Watson*

True valor lies in the middle,
    between cowardice and rashness.

*Miguel de Cervantes*

Too much ambition is a bad thing to have
in a bunker.

*Bobby Jones*

Never let one bad shot disrupt your rhythm
or concentration.

*Sam Snead*

There's a little boy in all of us. The trick
is knowing how to let that child come out.

*Mac O'Grady*

# Missing a short putt doesn't mean that I have to hit my next drive out-of-bounds.

*Tony Lema*

The object of golf is to beat someone. Make sure that someone is not yourself.

*Bobby Jones*

# LESSON 9: ACCEPTANCE
## *Play It Where It Lies*

After a particularly poor round at Walton Heath, Valentine Viscount Castlerosse instructed his caddie, "Have the clubs destroyed, and leave the course." Every golfer knows the feeling. As Thomas Boswell observed, "The game of golf was created with humiliation in mind."

Because the game of golf is an exercise in humility, it is wonderful training for life. The thoughtful golfer comes to understand that hazards and bad bounces are simply part of the game. The best thing we can do about our tough breaks is to face them with determined acceptance. And play them where they lie.

You can't get too keyed up about the bounces a golf ball takes.

*Greg Norman*

# The game isn't fair, but then life isn't fair either.

*Lee Trevino*

Every day on the golf course is about
making little adjustments, taking what
you've got on that day and finding
the way to deal with it.

*Tiger Woods*

Strengthen yourself with contentment
for it is an impregnable fortress.

*Epictetus*

Little minds have little worries.
Big minds have no room for worries.

*Ralph Waldo Emerson*

Accept your disappointments and triumphs
equally.

*Harvey Penick*

Good times, bad times.
They're both hard to grasp.

*Roger Maltbie*

If I could only learn to react differently
between the green and the next tee box
after I have a bad hole.

*Jim Thorpe*

Some players never learn to accept
misfortune. You have to remember that
you're not God's only child of misfortune.

*Joe Inman*

A pessimist is one who makes difficulties
of his opportunities. An optimist is one who
makes opportunities of his difficulties.

*Harry Truman*

Like life, golf is a game of good breaks and
   bad breaks. There is nothing fair about it.

*Harvey Penick*


Golf is not a fair game and
         was never meant to be.

*Jack Nicklaus*


Momentum swirls. Golf is not a fair game.
   It's a rude game.

*Fuzzy Zoeller*


There is only one way to happiness and
   that is to cease worrying about things
   which are beyond the power of our will.

*Epictetus*

# We must all play the ball as we find it.

*Bobby Jones*

# Golf spelled backwards is flog.

*Glen Waggoner*

Golf is a game of mistakes.

*Sam Snead*

Self-pity is our worst enemy and if we yield
to it, we can never do anything wise
in the world.

*Helen Keller*

Self-pity is the great masochistic tranquilizer.

*Jackie Gleason*

Accept the consequences.
The ball is either going to drop or it isn't.

*Fred Couples*

You can't hate yourself for finishing second.

*Fuzzy Zoeller*

Golf acts as a corrective against sinful pride.
If Cleopatra had been ousted in the first round
of the Ladies' Singles, we should have heard a
lot less of her proud imperiousness.

*P. G. Wodehouse*

Golf is the hardest game in the world.
There's no way you can ever get it. Just when
you think you do, the game jumps up
and puts you in your place.

*Ben Crenshaw*

No matter how poorly you play, there is
always someone you can beat. No matter how
well you play, there is always someone
who can beat you.

*Harvey Penick*

Golf is an unmasterable game.
That knowledge is the key to being a master.

*Thomas Boswell*

I'm learning to take the bad days better.
This isn't a matter of life and death.

*Dottie Mochrie*

Walter Hagen would play a succession
of holes as though divinely inspired. Then
from a clear sky would come a stroke of
unbelievable inaccuracy — a wild slice, or a
top, or a quick, semi-circular hook — and the
heart of the duffer warmed to the god that
could descend to the level of man.

*Henry Longhurst*

Only a mediocre person is always
at his best.

*Somerset Maugham*

There comes a time when you realize
you can't fly it over every fairway bunker.

*Jack Nicklaus*

Once a time is past, it's past. I have to look
to the future. I have to see what skills I have
now. I can't look backwards, because that
man doesn't exist anymore.

*Jack Nicklaus*

Fear not for the future, weep not for the past.

*Percy Bysshe Shelley*

Golf brings out your assets and liabilities
as a person.

*Hale Irwin*

Don't try to overhaul your basic personality
in order to play better golf.
It won't work.

*Sam Snead*

To play competitive golf you must be
determined, yet resigned.

*Thomas Boswell*

I've lost balls in every
hazard and on every
course I've tried, but
when I lose a ball in the
ball washer, it's time
to take stock.

*Milton Gross*

# LESSON 10: APPRECIATION
## *Enjoy the Round*

Link St. Clair wrote, "The essence of golf is more than a game; it's a philosophy of life." One of golf's most endearing philosophers was the inimitable Walter Hagen. Hagen instructed his playing partners to "stop and smell the roses." We would all do well to follow that advice. Golf, after all, is still a game. If we fail to enjoy it, we have no one to blame but ourselves.

The next time you tee it up, take a long moment to consider your good fortune. Smell the freshly cut grass. Look carefully at the beautiful scenery. Enjoy the moment. Because in golf, as in life, no one smells the roses for you.

Golf, like life, should be enjoyable.

*John Daly*

Do you play to enjoy golf or do you enjoy
yourself while you play golf?

*Chuck Hogan*

Golf courses are the answer to the world's
problems. When I get out on that green carpet
called a fairway and manage to poke the ball
right down the middle, my surroundings look
like a touch of heaven on earth.

*Jimmy Demaret*

I love golf, but golf is no longer at the top
of my priority list. Golf is no longer my god.

*Paul Azinger*

# Playing golf is a privilege, not a sentence.

*Harvey Penick*

Take pleasure
not in the score,
but in the game.

*Bobby Jones*

Things can always be better,
 but they can also be worse. Why not look
 on the good side?

*Fuzzy Zoeller*

I believe playing golf can bring
 you happiness.

*Harvey Penick*

The clearest sign of wisdom
 is continued cheerfulness.

*Michel de Montaigne*

The facility for keeping oneself relaxed
at all times adds a great deal to the pleasure
of living.

*Bobby Locke*

Each day provides its own gifts.

*Martial*

Golf is the only game in which one can
perform on the very battleground on which
the mighty have made history. The humble
can stand exactly where the great man stood.
No one, broadly speaking, can play tennis at
Wimbledon or Forest Hills. Anyone can play
at St. Andrews tomorrow.

*Henry Longhurst*

On the golf course, a man may be the
dogged victim of inexorable fate, be struck
down by an appalling stroke of tragedy,
become the hero of unbelievable melodrama,
or the clown in a side-splitting comedy —
any of these within a few hours, and all
without having to bury a corpse
or repair a tangled personality.

*Bobby Jones*

Golf is going to test you, but the test
is a game.

*Tom Watson*

A round of golf should permit
eighteen inspirations.

*A. W. Tillinghast*

Little good comes from brooding about
mistakes. The next shot, in golf or in life,
is the big one.

*Grantland Rice*

# If the sun is up, why aren't you playing golf?

*Lee Trevino*

# Sources

# About Wisdom Books

Wisdom Books chronicle memorable quotations in an easy-to-read style. Written by Criswell Freeman, this series provides inspiring, thoughtful and humorous messages from entertainers, athletes, scientists, politicians, clerics, writers and renegades. Each title focuses on a particular region or area of special interest.

Combining his passion for quotations with extensive training in psychology, Dr. Freeman revisits timeless themes such as perseverance, courage, love, forgiveness and faith.

"Quotations help us remember the simple yet profound truths that give life perspective and meaning," notes Freeman. "When it comes to life's most important lessons, we can all use gentle reminders."

# About the Author

Criswell Freeman is a Doctor of Clinical Psychology living in Nashville, Tennessee. He is the author of *When Life Throws You a Curveball, Hit It* and *The Wisdom Series* from WALNUT GROVE PRESS.

# The Wisdom Series

*by Dr. Criswell Freeman*

## Regional Titles

| | |
|---|---|
| Wisdom Made in America | ISBN 1-887655-07-7 |
| The Book of Southern Wisdom | ISBN 0-9640955-3-X |
| The Wisdom of the Midwest | ISBN 1-887655-17-4 |
| The Wisdom of the West | ISBN 1-887655-31-X |
| The Book of Texas Wisdom | ISBN 0-9640955-8-0 |
| The Book of Florida Wisdom | ISBN 0-9640955-9-9 |
| The Book of California Wisdom | ISBN 1-887655-14-X |
| The Book of New York Wisdom | ISBN 1-887655-16-6 |
| The Book of New England Wisdom | ISBN 1-887655-15-8 |

## Sports Titles

| | |
|---|---|
| The Golfer's Book of Wisdom | ISBN 0-9640955-6-4 |
| The Putter Principle | ISBN 1-887655-39-5 |
| The Golfer's Guide to Life | ISBN 1-887655-38-7 |
| The Wisdom of Southern Football | ISBN 0-9640955-7-2 |
| The Book of Stock Car Wisdom | ISBN 1-887655-12-3 |
| The Wisdom of Old-Time Baseball | ISBN 1-887655-08-5 |
| The Book of Football Wisdom | ISBN 1-887655-18-2 |
| The Book of Basketball Wisdom | ISBN 1-887655-32-8 |
| The Fisherman's Guide to Life | ISBN 1-887655-30-1 |

## Special Interest Titles

| | |
|---|---|
| The Book of Country Music Wisdom | ISBN 0-9640955-1-3 |
| The Wisdom of Old-Time Television | ISBN 1-887655-64-6 |
| The Wisdom of the Heart | ISBN 1-887655-34-4 |
| The Guide to Better Birthdays | ISBN 1-887655-35-2 |
| The Gardener's Guide to Life | ISBN 1-887655-40-9 |
| Minutes from the Great Women's Coffee Club (by Angela Beasley) | ISBN 1-887655-33-6 |

Wisdom Books are available through booksellers everywhere.
For information about a retailer near you, call 1-800-256-8584.